follow me

You and Me

CAROLINE GRIMSHAW

World Book

in association with

TWOCAN

follow me and find out (almost) everything about people!

follow me

You and Me

CREATIVE AND EDITORIAL DIRECTOR
CONCEPT/FORMAT/DESIGN/TEXT
CAROLINE GRIMSHAW

SCIENCE CONSULTANT
JOHN STRINGER UNIVERSITY OF WARWICK, U.K.

TEXT EDITORS
IQBAL HUSSAIN AND **ROBERT SVED**

ILLUSTRATIONS
NICK DUFFY ◊ **SPIKE GERRELL**
CAROLINE GRIMSHAW

THANKS TO
LAURA CARTWRIGHT PICTURE RESEARCH
BRONWEN LEWIS EDITORIAL SUPPORT
PATRICIA OHLENROTH WORLD BOOK, INC.

TITLES IN THIS SERIES
◊ YOU AND ME
◊ OUR WORLD

FIRST PUBLISHED IN THE UNITED STATES AND CANADA BY
WORLD BOOK, INC.
525 W. MONROE
CHICAGO, IL 60661
IN ASSOCIATION WITH TWO-CAN PUBLISHING LTD.

COPYRIGHT © CAROLINE GRIMSHAW 1997

FOR INFORMATION ON OTHER WORLD BOOK PRODUCTS,
CALL 1-800-255-1750, EXT. 2238, OR VISIT US AT OUR WEB SITE AT
HTTP://WWW.WORLDBOOK.COM

GRIMSHAW, CAROLINE.
YOU AND ME / CAROLINE GRIMSHAW; SCIENCE CONSULTANT, JOHN
STRINGER.   P. CM. -- (FOLLOW ME)   INCLUDES INDEX.
SUMMARY: USES BRIEF TEXT, ILLUSTRATIONS, QUIZZES, AND GAMES TO
EXPLAIN ABOUT THE HUMAN BODY, EMOTIONS, FAMILIES, WORLD
POPULATION, AND PEACE.
ISBN 0-7166-8802-6 (HC). -- ISBN 0-7166-8803-4 (SC).
1. BODY, HUMAN-JUVENILE LITERATURE. 2. EMOTIONS-JUVENILE
LITERATURE. 3. DISEASES-JUVENILE LITERATURE. 4. COMMUNICATION-
JUVENILE LITERATURE. 5. POPULATION-JUVENILE LITERATURE. 6. PEACE-
JUVENILE LITERATURE. [1. BODY, HUMAN. 2. EMOTIONS. 3. POPULATION.]
I. TITLE. II. SERIES: FOLLOW ME (CHICAGO, ILL.)
QM27.G75 1997
612--DC21   97-9316

PRINTED IN SPAIN
1 2 3 4 5 6 7 8 9 10 01 00 99 98 97

Welcome to a special book all about You and Me

Meet your guides...

Hop

Take a giant hop with this bunny to Show Me panels. These activities will help you see for yourself that the facts you are reading are true. Look out for this hot spot:

 show me

Skip

Skip along to Tricky Test Time panels with this kangaroo. Here you will find puzzles, quizzes, and activities. The answers are on the last page of the book. Watch out for this hot spot:

 tricky test time

Jump

Take a looping leap with this flying fish. The Follow Me panels let you choose to move to a page further on in the book. This clever little fish will point out the links between you, your family, and all the people in the world. Follow the fish when you see this hot spot:

 follow me

Look out for all sorts of things hiding on the pages when you see this hot spot:

in hiding

What's inside...

You're just a Hop, Skip, and Jump away from knowing (almost) everything about people!

Genes **5**

Friends **17**

Messages **14**

Sleep **9**

Crowds **18**

Being sick **10**

Where should you start? Just choose a subject and turn to that page.

Take your pick and let's get going.
f⊚ll⊚w me

Feelings **12**

Twins **5**

Being scared **13**

Warmth **9**

Eyes **4**

Marriage **17**

Peace **20**

Clothes **15**

Being happy **12**

Disease **11**

Food **8**

Bones **6**

War **21**

Family **16**

Language **15**

Hair **4**

You're so

Special

Every person on the planet is different from every other.
Read on to find out how and why this is.

How are we all different?

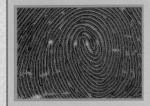

We all look different. Look at the people around you.

HAIR
What kind of hair have they got? Is it short, straight, wavy, or curly? What color is it?

SKIN
Is their skin freckly, pale, dark, or smooth? In the sun, your skin produces more of a substance called melanin, which causes light skin to tan or freckle.

EYES
What color are their eyes? Eyes may be blue, brown, green, hazel, or gray. Sometimes people's eyes are two different colors. What shape are their eyes?

tricky test time

Hair grows out of tiny holes in our skin. The shape of the hole affects whether the hair is straight or curly. Match the hair to the hole.

follow me

It is not just the way we look that makes us different. Follow me to page 22.

We all have different fingerprints.

The skin that covers the ends of your fingers has ridges called fingerprints. Even identical twins have different fingerprint patterns.

show me

Look closely at the fingerprints of five people you know. Are there any similar shapes?

follow me

Is some food good for our bodies and some bad? Follow me to page 8.

We are all different shapes and sizes.

The shape of our bodies depends on our genes, what we eat, and the exercise that we do. Take a look at this picture.

THE SUMO WRESTLER
Sumo wrestling is a popular Japanese sport. These wrestlers work hard to keep up their weight and size.

Why are we all different?

Your body is made up of millions of cells. Every person has many genes inside these cells. Genes are special instructions that control the way we look. Genes are passed on to us from each parent. You may look like your relatives because your cells contain many of the same gene instructions.

show me

Can you roll your tongue lengthwise? This is controlled by your genes – so if you can't, the chances are your parents can't either!

follow me

Do you want to find out what being in a family is all about? Follow me to page 16.

Are you a twin?

Identical twins come from the same egg inside their mother. The egg splits in half. So, when they are born, they have exactly the same genes.

tricky test time

Three children born together from the same mother are called triplets. How many people do you know if you know four pairs of twins and two sets of triplets?

in hiding

These two boys are identical twins. Find five pairs of identical twins hidden on these pages.

All about your

Amazing body

What are people made of? What
makes the body work? Find out here!

Making a human being

The body is made up of
millions of different parts.
They all fit together like a
huge puzzle, giving us life.

WHAT IS A PERSON MADE OF?
◊ About 208 bones
◊ About 650 muscles
◊ About 5 million strands of hair
◊ About 62,137 miles (100,000 kilometers) of blood vessels (tiny tubes that carry blood around your body)
◊ About 26 feet (8 meters) of intestines (tubes that your food passes through)
◊ Organs, such as the heart and brain
◊ A covering of skin
◊ And other bits and pieces!

in hiding

Can you find the
five different parts
of the body hiding
on these pages?

65%
of your body
is made up of
water. Half of
this is found
in the blood.
The rest is in
other parts
of the body.

follow me

What do you need to
stay alive? Follow me
to page 8 to find out.

tricky test time

X-ray photographs
can show you how
the inside of your
body looks. X rays
pass through skin
and muscle but not
through bone.
Which part of the
body does this X-ray
photograph show?

① Your bones

Bones support the body and also protect
the soft organs inside. We are born with
more bones than we die with. This
is because the bones of our skull have
joined together by the time we become
adults. Muscles are connected to the
bones so that we can move.

② Your skin

Skin covers your body. In some places, your skin is very thin, like your eyelids. Sometimes it is thick, like the soles of your feet.

 show me

Your body sheds millions of dead skin cells every day. Most of them end up as house dust!

Look carefully at this magnified photograph of skin. Then look at and feel your own skin. Are some places smoother than others?

 **follow me**

What can happen if you cut or scratch your skin? Follow me to page 11.

③ Your heart

Your heart is a powerful muscle. Each beat of your heart pumps the blood around your body.

 show me

How big is your heart? Clench your fist tightly. This is about the size of your heart!

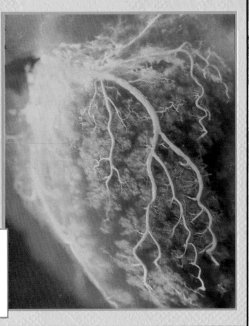

What does it mean to have special needs?

We know our bodies all look different. They may work in different ways too. Some people are born with special needs, which can mean that parts of their body do not work. They may have to find other ways to move around or to communicate with people.

Many buildings have ramps and sliding doors to help people in wheelchairs enter and exit.

④ Your brain

Your brain controls everything you do. You find out about the outside world by using your senses, such as sight and smell. These senses send messages to your brain, which acts on this information. The brain is also responsible for your feelings and memories.

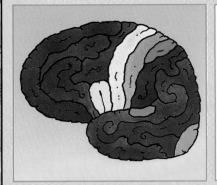

EXAMINE THIS DIAGRAM OF THE BRAIN

Each part of the brain has a particular job.

- ■ hearing
- □ talking
- ■ seeing
- ■ smelling
- □ moving
- ■ touching

 **tricky test time**

Find four things in this picture that would make it hard for a wheelchair-user to move around.

What's the most important thing in life?

Staying alive!

Read on and discover what we need to be healthy and happy.

① Food

Food keeps you warm. It gives you energy and can keep your body in tip-top condition.

FOOD HAS LOTS OF GOOD THINGS IN IT TO KEEP YOU HEALTHY:

1 CARBOHYDRATES are a main supply of energy.
2 PROTEINS help the body grow and repair itself.
3 VITAMINS AND MINERALS help keep the body in good working order.
4 FATS are used to build parts of the body and give you energy.

What should you eat?

It is very important to eat a balanced diet so that you have all the nutrients you need to stay healthy. You should cut down on sugar and fat and eat more fruits and vegetables.

follow me

Why do we sometimes feel sick? Follow me to page 10.

tricky test time

Follow the lines from the food to see what stays on the plate. Foods that you should try to eat less of have paths leading away from the plate.

in hiding

Can you spot the fruit and sweets hidden on these pages?

②Drink

You need to drink because your body loses water when you breathe, when you sweat, and when you urinate.

show me

See how you sweat on a hot day after exercising. Do you feel thirsty afterwards?

④Sunlight

You need sunlight to make vitamin D, which is important for your body. It also affects a tiny part of the brain called the pineal gland, which helps keep you feeling happy.

Too much sun can cause wrinkles and even skin cancer. Sunscreen lotions help protect the skin.

③Sleep

You need sleep because it lets your body save energy and repair itself.

tricky test time

An American, Robert MacDonald, holds the record for staying awake. To find out how many days he went without sleep, figure out the answer to this problem: $2 \times 4 + 10 = ?$

LIVING IN THE COLD
Inuits can survive in very low temperatures. One reason is their diet, which is rich in protein and fat. Proteins and fats help protect their bodies from the cold.

⑤Warmth

People are warm-blooded, which means that their body temperature stays much the same no matter how hot or cold it is around them. But extreme changes in temperature can seriously damage the body.

⑥Love

You need love, friends, and lots of encouragement.

follow me

Friends know you.
Who else knows you?
Follow me to page 16.

Sick

Your body doesn't work properly all the time. Find out some reasons why you may feel sick and how you can get better.

This photograph shows a person who is sick. Have you ever been too sick to leave your bed?

Why do we sometimes feel sick?

Your body is always being attacked by germs. There are two main kinds of germs: bacteria (which can grow both inside and outside your body) and viruses (which can only grow inside your body). What does a germ look like? This!

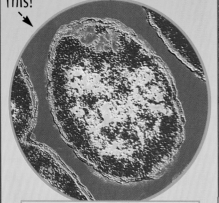

This photograph of bacteria has been enlarged. If 10,000 were placed end to end, they would measure about a third of an inch (1 centimeter).

in hiding

Can you spot the four things hidden on these pages that can make you very sick?

show me

Bacteria grow in wet places. Leave two pieces of bread, one wet and one dry, in separate, sealed plastic bags. You'll see that the wet bread goes moldy first. Throw the bags away afterward – unopened.

tricky test time

Bacteria grow by splitting in two. One bacteria splits every 20 minutes. If you start off with just one, how many bacteria will there be after two hours?

Although your body has special ways of keeping out germs, you also need to wash regularly to keep yourself clean.

HOW DO GERMS INVADE YOUR BODY?

1 THROUGH CUTS AND SCRATCHES
If you prick yourself on a rusty nail, you may become infected.

2 BREATHING IN
One quart (liter) of air has about one million bacteria. Most are harmless. But some harmful germs, such as those that cause colds and coughs, might enter your body when you breathe.

3 INSECT BITES
A mosquito spreads a disease called *malaria* by piercing a person's skin. The germ enters the body through the hole.

4 FOOD AND DRINK
Rotten eggs and meat carry germs that can cause food poisoning.

follow me

What happens when people do not have enough food? Follow me to page 19 to find out.

How can we fight disease?

Your body tries hard to get rid of harmful germs. But sometimes it can't fight back on its own, and you may need medical help. Doctors are specially trained to recognize diseases and suggest a cure. One of the first doctors that we know of was called Imhotep. He worked in ancient Egypt more than 4,600 years ago.

ANTIBIOTICS
When your body has an infection, you may have to take an antibiotic. This is medicine, usually in the form of pills, that kills bacteria. A very important antibiotic called *penicillin* was discovered in 1928 by the scientist Alexander Fleming.

ALTERNATIVE MEDICINE
People all over the world have different ways of fighting disease. Many treat the body without using drugs or surgery.

With acupuncture, sharp needles are pushed through the skin at certain points. People think this helps the body's energy to flow properly.

VACCINES
To stop you from catching serious diseases, you may receive a vaccine. A vaccine is a small amount of a weakened virus that usually is injected into the body. Your body makes special substances to fight the virus. That way, it is prepared for the real thing in the future.

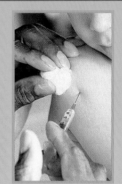

tricky test time

Make your way through this true (**T**) or false (**F**) maze to learn more about vaccines.

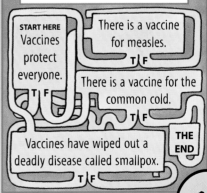

START HERE
Vaccines protect everyone.
T | F

There is a vaccine for measles.
T | F

There is a vaccine for the common cold.
T | F

Vaccines have wiped out a deadly disease called smallpox.
T | F

THE END

11

All about your

Feelings

You have feelings, or emotions, about everything that happens to you. For example, you can feel love, fear, anger, surprise, or pride. Your emotions are often mixed. You might feel both surprised and happy, or sad and angry.

① ANGRY   ② HAPPY

in hiding

Can you find the faces hidden on these pages? What feeling does each face show?

① What makes you angry?

When you are angry, you may want to shout at someone, or even hurt them, because you feel that they have been unfair or cruel. You may feel angry at yourself or at a situation, such as getting a flat tire on your bicycle.

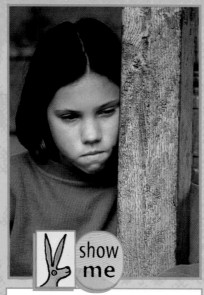

show me

Getting angry does not usually make you feel better. Next time you feel upset, try to calm down by slowly counting to ten. Take deep breaths. If you can, walk away from whomever, or whatever, is making you feel angry.

follow me

Follow me to page 21 to find out why wars happen.

② What makes you happy?

Everyone has different things that make them happy. Some people feel happy when they are outside on a sunny day. Others feel happier staying indoors watching television. You may like to do both things at different times!

Laughter is our way of letting go when we find something funny.

(3) SAD

(4) SCARED

follow me

Faces are not the only part of the body that show how you are feeling. Follow me to page 14 to find out about body language.

(4) What makes you scared?

People can be scared of many things, including loud noises, the dark, and dangerous situations.

PHOBIAS
A phobia is when you have an unreasonable fear of one particular thing.
◊ Arachnophobia is a fear of spiders.
◊ Claustrophobia is a fear of being in small spaces.

WHAT HAPPENS TO YOUR BODY WHEN YOU ARE SCARED?
◊ You go pale.
◊ Your heart beats faster.
◊ Your breathing speeds up.

tricky test time

You can often tell how someone is feeling by the look on his or her face. People all over the world share many similar expressions. Match the words to the emotions shown on the faces.

 1
 2
 3
 4

FEAR SURPRISE
SADNESS HAPPINESS

(3) What makes you sad?

If you feel confused, hurt, or alone, you may feel sad too, and sometimes you cry.

WHERE DO TEARS COME FROM?
Your eyes make tears all the time. Tears are a salty liquid for washing your eyes. When you cry, your eyes make more liquid than normal, and tears start to run down the inside corners of your eyes.

EXAMINE THIS DIAGRAM OF THE EYE.

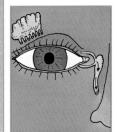

Tear glands make tears, which contain saltwater and chemicals to fight bacteria.
Tear ducts are tiny tubes that carry liquid from the eye to the nose.

Everybody sends

Messages

People show each other how they feel and what they think. This is called communicating. How do you communicate?

Your body gives you away.

The way you sit, stand, and move tells people a lot about how you are feeling. This is called your body language.

How you look and what you say are both ways of telling people how you feel.

show me

People with their arms crossed may not realize it, but they could be trying to tell you something! Look at this photograph. How do you think the person in the picture is feeling?

① Hair

The hairstyle you choose will depend on your taste, the fashion of the time, and what you are trying to say about yourself. This photograph was taken in 1976. The teenager has dyed his hair and then molded it into spikes. This style was called "punk."

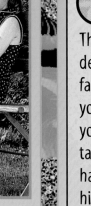

② Jewelry

Some people use jewelry, such as pins, bracelets, earrings, and necklaces, to decorate their bodies. A ring may be worn to show others that a person is married. Some wear pendants to show what religion they believe in.

③ Clothes

You choose your clothes because of their style and color and how comfortable they are. Many people wear clothes that are in fashion, which means that style of clothing is popular at the time. Some people have other reasons…

 tricky test time

Who is saying what?

A

"The clothes I wear suit the climate of the place that I live in."

1

B

"In my religion, Islam, women are advised to cover their heads."

2

C

"I'm covering my head to protect myself from the sun."

3

 **follow me**

How do we all manage to get along with each other? Follow me to page 20.

in hiding

Find the five items of clothing hidden on these pages.

You use language.

Language can be either spoken or written down. We use language to tell each other how we feel and what we believe. There are about 3,000 different languages spoken around the world.

All languages sound different. Punjabi has no "v" sound. The French roll their "r's". Swahili is full of clicks and whistles.

 tricky test time

Find out how many people speak these languages by solving these problems:

MANDARIN CHINESE $1{,}000 \text{ MILLION} - 175 \text{ MILLION} = ?$

ENGLISH $230 \text{ MILLION} + 200 \text{ MILLION} = ?$

HINDI $300 \text{ MILLION} + 25 \text{ MILLION} = ?$

SPANISH $520 \text{ MILLION} - 200 \text{ MILLION} = ?$

Language sounds are not all written down in the same way. Most languages have an alphabet for all the different sounds, while others, such as Chinese, have symbols for different words. In ancient Egypt, people drew pictures called hieroglyphics to get their message across.

 **show me**

Symbols may be used instead of words. Those shown here stand for recycling, a telephone, and male and female. They are recognized around the world.

1

2

3

Have you ever thought about

Who knows you?

You speak to different people every day. Your connections with other people are called relationships.

show me

Make a chart showing the people you see or talk to every day, about twice a week, twice a month, and once a year. This chart shows most of your relationships.

① Your family knows you.

tricky test time

The people in a family are usually related to each other by birth. There are many other different kinds of families. Some families include special friends and pets.

NUCLEAR FAMILY
Mother, father, children live together.

SINGLE-PARENT FAMILY
Children live with one parent and may visit the other parent.

EXTENDED FAMILY
Parents, children, and other relatives live together.

In some countries, especially poorer ones, people may choose to have a lot of children because many die young. Parents want to make sure that enough children survive to work for the family.

Can you solve this family riddle? A girl looks at a photograph and says, "This woman's son is my mother's husband." Who is the woman in the photograph? Is it:

1 The girl's aunt?

2 The girl's mother?

3 The girl's grandmother?

follow me

Members of a family who live far apart can still talk to each other. Follow me to page 23 to find out how.

in **hiding**

Find the families. There are four hidden on these pages.

What is marriage?

When a man and a woman decide to live together as husband and wife, they have a ceremony and make a promise to each other. This is marriage.

Most Christians have their marriage ceremony, or wedding, inside a church.

Hindu, Muslim, and Sikh parents may decide whom their children will marry.

 tricky test time

In South Korea in 1992, a record number of marriages took place at the same time. Figure out how many couples were married:
$2 \times 2 \times 5 \times 10 \times 10 \times 10 = ?$

② Your special friends know you.

A friend is someone you are fond of, trust, and enjoy spending time with. Friends often like the same things.

 follow me

How many people are there on the planet? Follow me to page 18 to find out.

③ People who you live, play, and study with know you.

Look at this photograph of people playing. All these people know each other in some way. If they like each other and have similar hobbies, they may become good friends.

Let's look at the

Crowded planet

Discover how many people there are on the Earth, where they all live, and how the planet supports all these people.

How many people?

The number of people living in a place is called the population. The population of the world is about 5.8 billion (5,800 million) – and it is increasing by 170 people every minute! Experts believe that in 40 years, the population will be more than 10 billion.

 show me

Look at this chart to discover how the world's population has grown in the past and how it is expected to grow in the future.

YEAR	MILLIONS OF PEOPLE
1900	1,633
1940	2,295
1980	4,450
2050	11,600

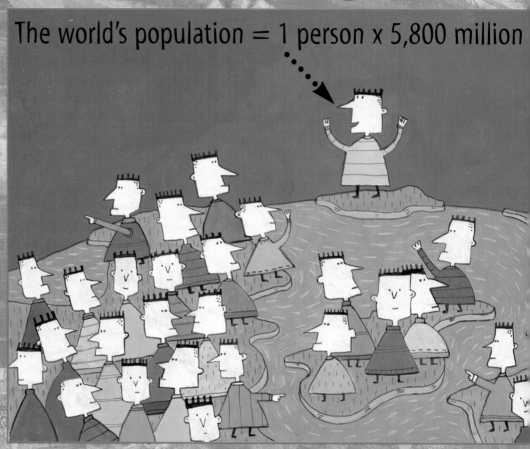

The world's population = 1 person x 5,800 million

Where do the people live?

Some places are very crowded. Others are not. Nearly a quarter of the world's population lives in one country – China! Other countries, such as Australia, are huge but have large areas of desert where few people live.

China has the largest population of any country in the world.

in hiding

There are ten tiny planets hidden on these pages. Can you find them?

Can the planet look after all these people?

IS THERE ENOUGH ROOM?

In some countries, space is a real problem. Towns and cities are especially crowded because many people go there to find work. Bombay, the largest city in India, has become so crowded that a new city has been built nearby so that people have more space to live comfortably.

India's population has doubled in the last 30 years.

IS THERE ENOUGH FOOD?

That depends on where you are. Enough food is grown for everyone in the world, but it is not spread around evenly. In most countries, there are some people who cannot afford to buy all the food they need.

follow me

Who looks after the countries of the world? Follow me to page 20 to find out.

Hot countries, such as Ethiopia and Sudan in Africa, have very little rain. So, crops don't always grow and people sometimes starve. Some richer countries try to help poorer countries by giving them food and showing the people how to grow more crops.

Why do people move around?

If people are looking for food or work, they sometimes move to a different town or country. These people are called *migrants*.

In 1996, hundreds of thousands of people fled from Rwanda in east Africa. They were afraid of the fighting taking place there. These people are called refugees.

tricky test time

Match the countries to their populations.

250 million

CHINA

USA

950 million

AUSTRALIA

1.2 billion

18 million   INDIA

People must look after the planet.

As the number of people in the world increases, more factories are built and more cars are made. These pollute the air with their fumes. The garbage that we throw away may end up polluting huge landfill sites. All these things harm our planet.

19

Keeping the
Peace

People all over the world have different ideas and opinions. From places as small as a school to places as large as a whole country, groups of people are chosen to try to help everyone get along.

Who keeps the peace?

1 GROUPS THAT LOOK AFTER ONE COUNTRY

In most countries, everyone has a say on who rules the country. People take part in elections to vote for a group of people who will rule. This group is called a government.

2 GROUPS THAT LOOK AFTER A FEW COUNTRIES

In Europe, an organization called the European Union (EU) was set up among European countries to promote cooperation in a number of areas, including politics and economics.

3 GROUPS THAT LOOK AFTER THE WORLD

Most countries of the world belong to a group called the United Nations (UN). This group tries to keep peace between countries and helps them solve their problems.

These people are voting in an election.

 follow me

How can we find out more about each other? Follow me to page 23.

In 1995, UN soldiers were sent to keep the peace in Bosnia.

Why do wars happen?

WARS

If a country decides that it wants to have power over certain people and land, it may start a fight called a war.

tricky test time

In 1896, the shortest war ever was fought. Use the clocks to figure out how long this war between Britain and Zanzibar lasted.

THE WAR STARTED THE WAR ENDED

Wars harm the planet and many people lose their lives. Between 1939 and 1945, about 55 million people died in World War II. This is almost twice as many people as now live in all of Canada.

How can we look after each other?

GIVING TO PEOPLE IN NEED

Charities are organizations set up to persuade people who have enough to give to those who have very little. Money, food, clothes, and medicine are sent to people in need. Charities may also help farmers by giving them tools, improving the water supply, and training them to make better use of their land.

On July 13, 1985, over 1½ billion people around the world turned on their televisions to watch two special concerts held in England and America. People were asked to give money to help those starving in Africa. Millions of dollars were raised. This event was called "Live Aid".

in hiding

Can you find the three different flags hidden on these pages?

What's the Difference

People live and work together in groups called communities. These communities have their own special ways of living and surviving. Look at these different groups.

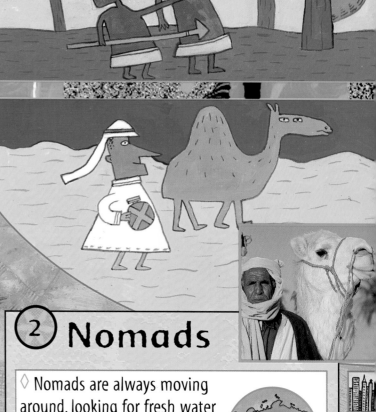

① Hunter-gatherers

◇ Hunter-gatherers hunt for meat and gather nuts, fruits, and wild plants in the forest.
◇ The Pygmies, who live in central Africa, are hunter-gatherers.
◇ They live in groups of about 100. They do not have a leader. Instead, they solve problems by talking about them as a group.
◇ Their homes are small huts made of branches and leaves.

Almost 80 percent of the world's people are farmers; 20 percent live in towns; less than 1 percent are nomads and hunter-gatherers.

② Nomads

◇ Nomads are always moving around, looking for fresh water and places where their camels and sheep can graze.
◇ The Bedouins, who live in the deserts of the Middle East, are nomads.
◇ Bedouins travel in groups of between 50 and 500, and may travel as far as 600 miles (1,000 km) in a year!
◇ They live in tents, which are easy to carry from place to place.

③ Farmers

◊ Farmers grow crops and raise animals.

◊ Rice farmers in southern China spend their days working in the water-filled rice fields.

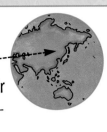

◊ Rice farmers may live in large communities. Some family groups live in bamboo houses, built on legs called stilts.

④ City dwellers

◊ City dwellers live in busy, crowded cities, such as New York City.

◊ Cities are full of large and small communities. They include people who have moved there from other parts of the world.

◊ Many people work for much of the week and relax on the weekend.

◊ Because there is a shortage of space, many people in cities live in large, high-rise apartment buildings.

in hiding

Can you find the bow and arrow, camel, skyscraper, and water buffalo hidden on these pages? Which groups of people do they belong to?

HOW CAN WE FIND OUT MORE ABOUT EACH OTHER?

◊ We can travel around the world.

◊ We can watch television and read newspapers and books.

◊ We can talk to people from other countries. When people move from one country to another, they bring with them new ideas about the world.

Today, people on different sides of the world can easily communicate with each other. They can mail a letter or use the telephone. Fax machines and computers can send messages in just a few minutes.

show me

Make a note of the different telephone calls your family makes or letters your family sends in a week. What is the farthest they have ever sent a message?

So that's the end of your journey. Now you know (almost) everything about people!

follow me You and Me

Index

tricky test time

THE ANSWERS P4: round hole = straight hair; oval hole = wavy hair; oblong hole = curly hair. P5: 14 people. P6: hand. P7: stairs; narrow doorways; clutter on floor; open filing cabinets blocking the way. P8: foods we should eat less of = cakes, red meat, butter, chocolate, french fries; foods we should eat more of = beans, fish, apples, broccoli, chicken, flour. P9: 18 days. P10: 64 bacteria. P11: F - vaccines do not work for 1 in 10 people; T; T; F - a vaccine is difficult to make, because the cold virus keeps changing its shape. P13: 1 = fear; 2 = sadness; 3 = surprise; 4 = happiness. P15: (left) A2; B3; C1; (right) Mandarin Chinese = 825 million; English = 430 million; Hindi = 325 million; Spanish = 320 million. P16: the girl's grandmother. P17: 20,000 couples. P19: China = 1.2 billion; India = 950 million; USA = 250 million; Australia = 18 million. P21: the war started at 9:02 a.m. and ended at 9:40 a.m., lasting 38 minutes. P23: fried worms = Botswana; grasshopper kebabs = Burma; kangaroo steaks = Australia; pickled snails = France.